Anthems

11 anthems for mixed voices

Contents

The accompanied items are all available in versions with orchestra. Instrumentation is shown at the foot of the relevant first pages. Full scores and instrumental parts are available on hire from the publisher.

MUSIC DEPARTMENT

OXFORD

UNIVERSITY PRESS

God be in my head

Words from the Sarum Primer

JOHN RUTTER

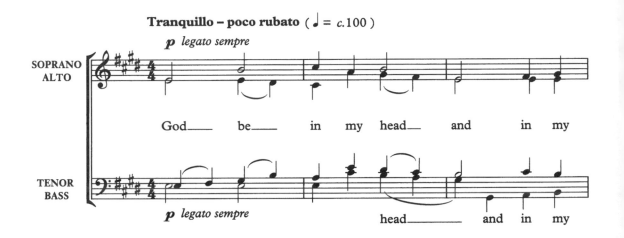

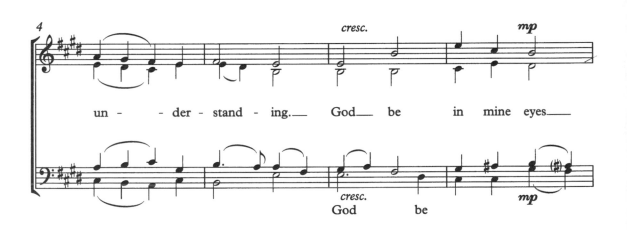

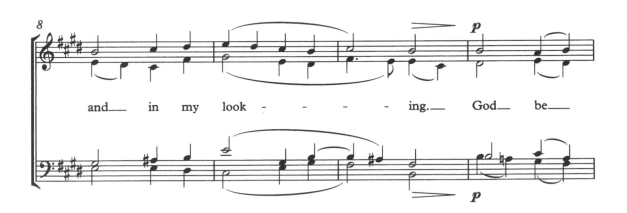

A Prayer of Saint Patrick

Words from
Saint Patrick's Breastplate (5th century)
Translated by Mrs C. F. Alexander (1823–95)

JOHN RUTTER

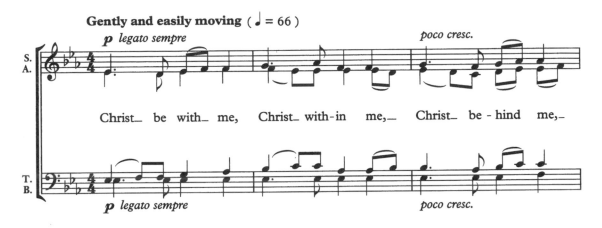

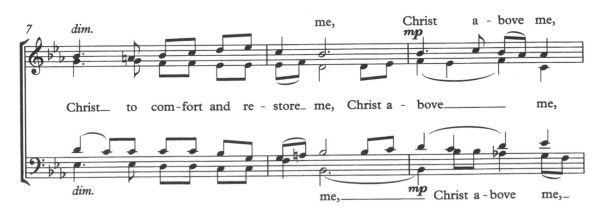

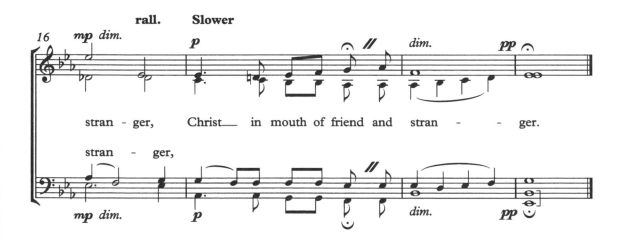

All things bright and beautiful

Words by Mrs C. F. Alexander (1823–95)

JOHN RUTTER

Also available for unison voices, with optional second part (U162). Instrumentation: 2fl, 2ob, 2cl, bsn, 2hn, perc, hp, str

*or hum, at conductor's discretion

All things wise and won-der-ful,— The Lord God made them all.—

He gave us eyes— to see— them, And lips that we— might tell————— How

all— things well.—

great is God Al - might - y,— Who has made all things well.

for Rosemary Heffley and the Texas Choral Directors' Association

For the beauty of the earth

Words by F. S. Pierpoint (1835–1917)

JOHN RUTTER

Also available in a two-part version (SS or SA) (T113). Instrumentation: 2fl, ob, 2cl, bsn, 2hn, perc, hp, str

This our joy - ful hymn_ of praise.

our hymn of praise.

our hymn of praise.

our hymn of praise.

for the Royal School of Church Music

I will sing with the spirit

I Corinthians 14, v.15

JOHN RUTTER

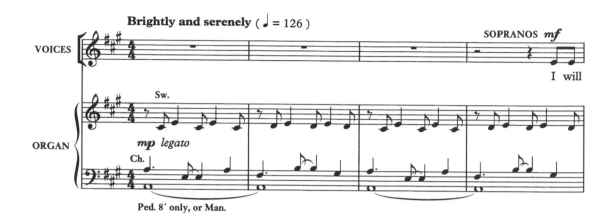

Also available for 2-part voices (E162). Instrumentation: 2fl, ob, 2cl, bsn, 2hn, str

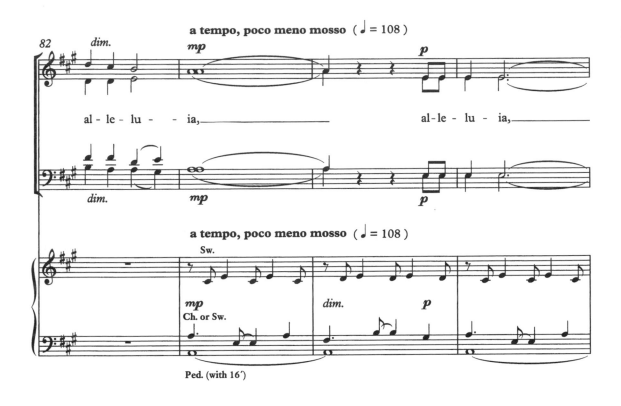

in celebration of the 70th anniversary of the Council for the Protection of Rural England

Look at the world

for children's choir (unison) and/or mixed choir (SATB)

Words and music by
JOHN RUTTER

*The accompaniment is more suitable for piano, but it can be played on the organ.

Instrumentation: 2fl, ob, 2cl, bsn, 2hn, hp, str

Look at the world: so ma-ny joys and won-ders,

So ma-ny mi-ra-cles a-long our way.

A

SOPRANOS (and CHILDREN)

ALTOS

Praise to thee, O Lord, for all cre - - a - tion,

TENORS

BASSES

(Ped.)

* Small notes in the accompaniment should be played for unison performances (without A. T. B. singers).

F ALL VOICES *f*

4. Ev-'ry good gift, all that we need and che-rish

Comes from the Lord — in to-ken of his love;

(TENORS and BASSES) *mf*

We are his hands, stew-ards of all his boun-ty;

(SOPRANOS and ALTOS)

His is the earth, and his the heav'ns a - bove:

Praise to thee, O Lord, for all cre - a - tion,

Give us thank - ful hearts, that we may see:

for Tim Brown and the choir of Clare College, Cambridge

Go forth into the world in peace

Words from the
Book of Common Prayer (1928)

JOHN RUTTER

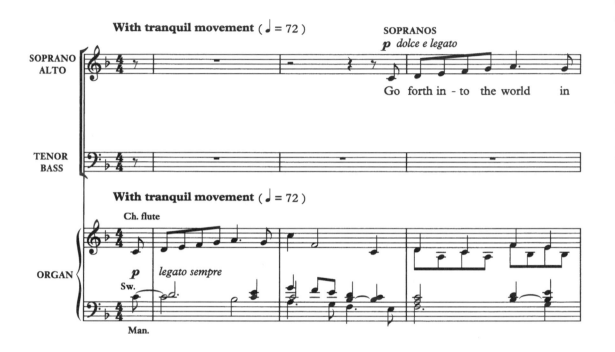

Instrumentation: strings

for Clare College, Cambridge

A Clare Benediction

Words and music by
JOHN RUTTER

Also available for SATB unaccompanied (E166), for SSA (W138), and for unison or two-part voices (U172)
Instrumentation: 2fl, ob, 2cl, bsn, 2hn, hp, str

sleep, may his an-gels watch o-ver you;_____ when you wake, may he fill you with his grace:_____ May you love him and serve him all your_ days, Then in hea-ven_____ may you see_____ his face.

in memoriam Edward T. Chapman

The Lord bless you and keep you

Numbers 6, v.24

JOHN RUTTER

Also available for SA (T119). Instrumentation: strings

10

S. *p dolce sempre*

you.

A.

The Lord bless you and keep you:_____ The

T.

B. *p dolce sempre*

13

Lord make his face to shine up-on you, to shine up - on you and be

mp

16

gra - cious,_____

gra - - cious, and be gra - cious un - to you:

The

gra - cious

gra - - cious, and be gra - - cious un - to you:

mp cresc.

for Bishop Thomas McMahon and the people of the Diocese of Brentwood

The peace of God

Book of Common Prayer (1662)
based on Philippians 4, v.7

JOHN RUTTER

Also available for SSA (W110). Instrumentation: strings

A Choral Amen

JOHN RUTTER